THOUGHTS TO HEAL YOUR SOUL

THOUGHTS
TO
HEAL
YOUR SOUL

*Poems and stories of Living with
Parkinson's Disease, Human Condition, Tragedies,
and Resilience*

Gilbert Luna Sierra

Many Seasons Press | Mesa, Arizona | 2022

FIRST EDITION

Thoughts to Heal Your Soul
Poems and stories of Living with Parkinson's Disease,
Human Condition, Tragedies, and Resilience

Published by Many Seasons Press
An imprint of Multimedia Publishing Project
PO Box 50553
Mesa, Arizona 85208-0028
480-939-9689 | MultimediaPublishingProject.com

Cover & book interior designed by Yolie Hernandez

ISBN: 978-1-956203-03-5

Library of Congress Control Number: 2022903661

Printed in the United States of America.

CONTENTS

PURPOSE

THE PURPOSE OF THIS BOOK is to draw attention to some human tragedy experiences and their effects on the people experiencing them. I hope to draw us all into the realm of a world lived by others in the hopes that we might gain compassion for those not as fortunate as some of us. It is easy to ignore the suffering of others because it is not in front of us, but at the very least I hope these poems will inspire you to pray for all the human tragedy experienced by others.

These poems are about real people, real-life experiences. Human tragedies such as racial discrimination, government genocide in El Salvador, COVID-19, and my personal experience of being diagnosed with, and living with Parkinson's disease. Throughout the years, the human tragedy experiences I witnessed in person or on the television formulated my values and compassion for humanity. I invite you to take this journey with love in your heart and allow these thoughts to heal your soul. As the first song/poem in this book says: "Come along now if you dare to see the world through my eyes."

HUMAN TRAGEDY, PAIN AND SORROW

GREENER SIDE OF THE TRACKS

THE YEAR 1985 WAS ONE OF THE WORST YEARS of the Salvadoran Civil War. The Salvadoran security forces and the death squads linked to them were abusing and massacring the civilian population. Many people fled the country fearing for their lives.

In the summer of 1985, thirteen desperate El Salvadoran refugees fled their country and made it to the Arizona desert. A terrible human tragedy occurred in the desert on that hot summer day. All thirteen refugees died in the Arizona desert attempting to escape an imminent death in their home country. When I witnessed this story on the news, I cried and prayed for them. I questioned God why these people are subjected to such a hard and difficult life and we Americans aren't. The reality of this particular tragedy is that these people died without a voice. In my prayers, I vowed to them that I would be their voice. I vowed that I would speak for them. Welcome to the first chapter of human tragedy.

Greener side of the tracks

(1985)

Come along with me and travel to another world
Unfamiliar to the world
As we know it.
It was not their fault that they were born there
And we were not
So come along now if you dare
To see the world through my eyes.

I fear that you'll think I'm insane
If I tell you that I can feel their pain,
Why them and not me, I'm undeserving
To be born on the greener side of the tracks.

They live their lives wondering when they will die
And when they do will someone cry
Or will no one miss them?
I hear you cry, it hurts me as you slowly die
And I will miss you when you're gone,
I'll speak for you.

I fear that you'll think I'm insane

If I tell you that I can feel their pain

Why them and not me, I'm undeserving

To be born

On the greener side of the tracks.

JUST LIKE YOU OLD MAN

I WAS BORN AND RAISED IN A SMALL COPPER MINING TOWN in Arizona named Miami. This community has experienced a great deal of human tragedy and adversity throughout the years. Especially my father's generation, made up of Mexicans and Mexican Americans. In their youth and early adult years, they experienced racial discrimination, wage discrimination, school segregation, and even segregation in the church. They were punished for speaking Spanish on school property, and were not given the same quality of education as their white counterparts. Many men died from lung diseases from working in the mines, leaving widows to raise their children. Another tragedy of this community is that many people have died from cancer. The community of Miami was the victim of what is known as downwinders. The radiation from the nuclear tests that were done in Nevada in the late 1950s and early 1960s blew into our community, and many residents and family members have died of cancer as a result of this radiation exposure.

"Just Like You Old Man" is a song/poem about the many Mexican and Mexican American men I interacted with while growing up there. All of them told me the same story that their purpose in life was to sacrifice in the hard labor and dangerous working conditions in the mines so their children could go to college and have a better life than they had. They all had the same dream of their children contributing to a better world than they grew up in. Many of these men lost wives, mothers, fathers, and other family members to cancer throughout the years of their lives. I watched them being beaten down by their hard lives and tragedies. They all hid it well with their smiles, but I could see it in their eyes. They were hurting inside. This song/poem is for all those men who influenced my life and helped formulate my values, as I witnessed them in their golden years hoping they got it right. To all those "old men," your life's not in vain, for you touched me too, and I hope I can spread love just like you, old man.

Just like you Old Man

(1985)

I watched the old man

I heard him sigh

But I could not help but wonder why.

He's lived his life

So full and content

Now he sits and wonders,

He wonders where the time went.

He gave to the needy

He gave to the poor

He took less

So others, they could have more.

His friends said, "Live your own life,"

They said, "Live for today,"

But he knew there had to be a better way.

What do you say to a man so sad,

Who freely gave up all he had?

Your life's not in vain

For you touched me too

And I hope that I can

Spread love just like you,

Just like you old man.

His wife suffered so long

But she had a strong will,

He sold his house

To pay the doctor bills.

What do you say to a man so sad,

Who freely gave up all he had?

Your life's not in vain

For you touched me too

And I hope that I can

Spread love just like you

Just like you old man

Just like you,

Just like you old man.

FOR YOUR FELLOW MAN

T HIS SONG/POEM IS ABOUT THE JOURNEY of my personal relationship with God and his Son Jesus Christ. This work is in the chapter of human tragedy and pain because throughout my life, the story of Jesus Christ's suffering and dying on the cross hurts me deeply. The depth of pain this man endured is very difficult for me to cope with. Throughout my childhood, and even now as an adult, every Palm Sunday when the Passion of our Lord is read, I cry. I cry in the middle of Mass, but I can't help it. This is something that I feel deeply.

In the fifth grade, we were studying about natural resources around the world and I had an epiphany. I came to the conclusion that God created this world with different natural resources in different parts of the world. My claim was that God intended us to share these natural resources with each other instead of being greedy with them. My teacher was amazed that a fifth-grader could have such a deep insight into how things could/should be. Fast forward to 1985 when I wrote this song/poem with the theme of, *in order to live, one must die to self in service of others.*

For your fellow man

(1985)

When I first heard His voice
I was no more than a boy
Too young to understand,
His hand reached out to me
He was a gentle man
In an untamed land.

He said, Living means you have to die
Love and peace that's the reason why
If you want to know the key to peace
Then you've gotta learn to give,
You gotta learn to live
For your Fellow Man.

And then we took a walk
Beneath the desert sun
A chill came over me,
Please don't be afraid,
The pain you feel comes from across the sea.
She was an orphan child
And she died there all alone,
And it's hurting me.

And He said, Living means you have to die

Love and peace that's the reason why

If you want to know the key to peace

Then you gotta learn to give,

You gotta learn to live

For your fellow man.

That's when the soldiers came

And they nailed Him to a tree

Right there in front of me,

The tears rolled down His face

But I never heard Him cry

And then I watched Him die.

And He said, Living means you have to die

Love and peace that's the reason why

If you want to know the key to peace

Then you gotta learn to give

You gotta learn to live

For your fellow man,

For your fellow man.

WHAT CAN WE SAY

I HAD A DREAM ONE NIGHT that I was sitting on a couch with a starving Ethiopian child. I could see his ribs, his stomach was concave, and I could see his cheekbones with skin hanging off them. The thing about this dream is that it was more than a dream. I felt that I really was on that couch with that child. The boy looked up at me and asked me, "Why do I have to die"? I did not have an answer for him and I abruptly awoke and wrote this short song. Maybe in the future, I'll add to it.

What can we say

(1985)

What can we say
To the children that will die today?
What can we do
To make their hunger pangs just go away?

There's got to be a better way,
How'd we let it get this way?

What can we say
To the mothers who must watch their children die?
What can we do
To dry the tears that they will surely cry?

There's got to be a better way,
How'd we let it get this way?

SERGEANT DANNY RIOS

DANNY AND I BECAME VERY GOOD FRIENDS since the fifth grade when we first met. Music was our common bond and we played music together often. He played drums and I played guitar. Throughout the years we learned to communicate a message together with our music. We became one mind, one heart, one soul. I remember one night when we were performing, I felt a really strong guitar solo coming on, I tilted my head back, closed my eyes and heard Danny yell from the drum kit, "Hold on Gilly, I'm coming with you!" He laid down a roll and the music that ensued was magic. It was like he knew what I was going to do next. It was magical. We experienced many magical nights of music in our band.

Danny was a member of the local National Guard unit in Claypool, Arizona, a suburb of Miami. Danny was proud to serve in the National Guard. His unit was called out to serve in the Gulf War in the early 90s. His unit was a transportation unit. I don't think any soldier is prepared to see what they see in war, but Danny definitely was not ready to see death like he saw. If you recall, the Gulf War was more of an air warfare. Targets were located and destroyed by airstrikes. Danny's company drove up on convoys that had been bombed by airstrikes and saw charred bodies in the seats. He showed me pictures of convoys all blown up, black, with death abound. I immediately saw that distant look in his eyes and knew he would never be the same. I sensed he was hurting, but he pretended to be okay. I tried to heal him with music, but I couldn't reach him. He slowly slipped away.

There is not a day that goes by that I don't think of you, my brother. I miss you more than words can describe. I'm grateful for the time we had, the music we shared, and the dreams we pursued together. It is a privilege to honor you here today with this poem. I love you, my brother.

To Sergeant Danny Rios

(2021)

My dear brother Danny
I'm thinking of you today,
I remember our sophomore year
When we listened to Santana,
Abraxas for the first time.

We were amazed by the sound
Not knowing that it was that sound
That would bond us together
For the rest of our lives.

Throughout the years
We played music together
We expressed our joys, sorrows and pain
Through the music we shared.

Music is how we spoke to each other
Music is how we coped,
I still hear you in the music
I still feel you in the beat.

When you came back from war
I could see you were hurting

I could feel your pain
You pretended you were fine.

Your whole tour of duty
You drove upon death
The kind of death
That causes nightmares.

I tried to help you cope
Through music
The only way I knew how
But the pain was just too great.

I watched you slip away
Little by little,
I watched the light dimming
In a man so full of life.

My brother, my friend
We were one heart and one soul
You shall live in me forever
I love you, my brother.

NIKKI ANN WHITE

(1990-1998)

NIKKI WAS AN EIGHT-YEAR-OLD second-grader who lost her battle with anaplastic astrocytoma. I never met Nikki but my then ten-year-old daughter brought her into my life. Janee came home one day and asked me for any loose change I might have. I asked her why and she told me that the daughter of the kindergarten teacher at her school had a brain tumor. Her last hope was an experimental treatment the medical insurance won't pay for it, so "we are going to pay for it." I was totally stunned to hear the conviction in this child's voice, that this group of children was going to help pay for this treatment with their lunch money, milk money, and by collecting cans. I was inspired and wrote a song to contribute to the cause, which I will discuss in the following paragraphs.

"Oh Children of God" (1998) — This poem is to express the feelings of inspiration that these children gave me. All the children involved in the "Nikki Project" truly believed they were going to save Nikki's life through their efforts. They worked hard and poured their hearts and souls into this project. You can hear their sincerity and conviction in the song "Nickels for Nikki."

"Nickels for Nikki" (1998) — I wrote this song because I was inspired by my ten-year-old daughter's conviction to help raise the money needed to pay for Nikki's treatment, and with the sole purpose of raising money for Nikki and her parents. My musician friends from Queen of Peace Catholic Church in Mesa, Arizona contributed their musical talents to this project. John Aranda, one of the musicians, was also the engineer and co-producer of the project. The song was recorded in his home recording studio. My Hispanic Children's Choir sang on this recording along with a couple of Janee's classmates. The local TV station Channel 3 came out to the studio and videotaped the Children's Choir, and presented the story on the morning news. To this day, when I listen to this song, I cry. I cry first because Nikki passed away, but also I cry because I can still hear the love, determination, conviction, and desire to help Nikki in the voices of children. At the end of the recording, I told the children to say whatever they wanted to say to Nikki. Those words coming from the children at the end of the song were not rehearsed. They were spontaneous feelings expressed in the moment.

"Little Angel" (1998) — One day, while working on the "Nickels for Nikki" project, I had a dream about Nikki. I dreamed that she was in a beautiful white dress and she asked me to dance with her. When I awoke the next morning I was so excited because I thought I had been given a vision that Nikki was going to live because I would be dancing with her at her wedding. That morning, I learned that Nikki had passed away. My heart was broken. I cried for hours. I sat down and wrote this song to express my feelings about Nikki Ann White. I never met Nikki, but she touched my heart and changed my life. Nikki, I think of you often and I look forward to when we will have that dance in heaven.

Oh Children of God

"Dad, if you really want to know about things
Ask a kid,"
So told me, a seven-year-old
Child of God.

"Dad, the insurance company won't pay for her treatment
So we are going to donate our lunch money,
milk money, and collect cans
And *we're* going to pay for her treatment,"
So told me that same Child of God at the age of ten.

Oh children of God
Once again you have opened my eyes and ears
So that I may see and hear
As you do.
Oh children of God
Once again you have opened my mind and heart
So that I may think and feel
As you do.

Oh children of God
Ambassadors of Hope
To you I wish to say

I envy your innocence

I respect your youthful wisdom

I admire your integrity

I salute your determination

I am inspired by your generosity

I am humbled by your honesty

I am touched by your selflessness

I am blessed by your presence,

God Bless You,

Oh Children of God.

Nickels for Nikki

When a little girl needs a helping hand
When a little girl needs a world that understands
Hey, little girl (Hey, little girl)
We want you to know (We want you to know)
We'll be there (We'll be there)
When a little girl feels alone and lives in fear
When a little girl sits and sheds a tear
Hey, little girl (Hey, little girl)
We want you to know (We want you to know)
We'll be there (We'll be there).

And we'll give Nickels for Nikki
Because we love you
We'll give Nickels for Nikki
Because we care
We'll give Nickels for Nikki
'Cause we believe in you
We'll give Nickels for Nikki
Because we care.

When her mom and dad try to pray
When her mom and dad can't find the words to say
Hey, mom and dad (Hey, mom and dad)

We want you to know (We want you to know)

We are here (We are here)

When the world seems so cold and cruel

When you can't find the help you need

Then come to our school

Hey, listen world (Hey, listen world)

We're not giving up (We're not giving up)

We are strong (We are strong)

When the future seems not so bright

We'll join together, we'll make it right

Hey, listen world (Hey, listen world)

We might be young (We might be young)

But we are strong (But we are strong).

And we'll give Nickels for Nikki

Because we love you

We'll give Nickels for Nikki

Because we care

We'll give Nickels for Nikki

'Cause we believe in you

We'll give Nickels for Nikki

Because we care.

Little angel

I never knew you, yet you touched my life
I never met you, but you still stole my heart
And as I try to understand
The goodness in God's plan
I look up to the sky
And know you're there.

Oh little angel, oh little angel
In the stars at night
I see the twinkle in your eyes
Oh little angel, oh little angel
After each cleansing rain
I see the colors of your smile
Oh little angel, oh little angel, oh little angel
Won't you smile for me?

I met you in my dream, you asked to dance with me,
I looked into your eyes, you became a part of me,
And as I try to understand
The goodness in God's plan
I look up to the sky
And know you're there.

Oh little angel, Oh little angel

In the stars at night

I see the twinkle in your eyes

Oh little angel, oh little angel

After each cleansing rain

I see the colors of your smile

Oh little angel, oh little angel, oh little angel

Won't you smile for me?

I understand the dream and when we'll have our dance

We'll meet in heaven, save that dance for me

And as I try to understand

The goodness in God's plan

I look up to the sky

And know you're there.

Oh little angel, oh little angel

In the stars at night

I see the twinkle in your eyes

Oh little angel, oh little angel

After each cleansing rain

I see the colors of your smile

Oh little angel, oh little angel, oh little angel

Won't you smile for me?

JOY

SONG FOR YOU, DAD

THIS IS A SONG I WROTE FOR MY DAD to show my appreciation for the love he gave me and the life lessons I learned from him. This song demonstrates how my Dad passed down his values to me. Besides giving me the gift of music by teaching me to play the guitar, he taught me how to be kind, loving, and respectful. My Dad was respected by his peers. He grew up in that era of poor treatment of Mexicans and Mexican Americans in Miami, Arizona, but he made sure to shelter me from that experience and encouraged me to not look back at what happened to him, but look forward and contribute to change. I am truly inspired by that man and I am pleased that I have the opportunity to honor him in this literary work.

Song for you, Dad

(1983)

This song's for you Dad
To try and say
Just what you mean to me
You've been an inspiration
In the things you say and do,
The things you say and do.

I remember when I was so young
And I stood in awe of you
With dedication to your cause
There is nothing you can't do,
Nothing you can't do.

You used to tell me
Point yourself ahead
Be the best man that you can
Others will try and put you down
But they can never change your heart
Treat others will respect
And so they will with you
Be not afraid to be yourself

Be proud of who you are.
My brothers and sister tell me
That I'm a lot like you
If that is true then I am proud
To be half the man you are.

Please know that when you do pass on
That you will never die
For I'll continue where you leave off
Cause I'm so much like you,
You know, I'm just like you.

You used to tell me
Point yourself ahead
Be the best man that you can
Others will try and put you down
But they can never change your heart
Treat others with respect
And so they will with you
Be not afraid to be yourself
Be proud of who you are.

These are a few things
I've learned from you
That helps me through each day.

Though there've been times when I let you down

You still believed in me

Thanks for guiding me

Thanks for loving me.

NEVER GONNA LET GO

I WROTE THIS SONG FOR MY WIFE JUANITA in our early years of marriage. I am presenting this piece in the Joy Chapter of this book because this song was prophetic. The line that says "We'll find strength in love, we can see this through" is so appropriate today. As you will read in the next chapter, I have been diagnosed with Parkinson's disease. This disease has brought about many changes in my life and causes many restrictions. The love that Juanita and I share gives us the strength to work through this time in our lives and yes, we will see this through. I love you even more now babe than I did when I wrote this song for you. That is really saying something because I remember the day I wrote this song for you. It was like they say, "I really had it bad."

Never gonna let go

(1978)

We were just fifteen
When we fell in love
You brought back the sunshine
Into my darkest days
You know you won my heart
From the beginning
My heart is bigger now
And it's filled with love for you.

And I'm never gonna let go, never gonna let go
Of these feelings that I have for you,
I only wanna show, I wanna make sure you know
That this love for you is forever.

I remember days
When all we had was each other, baby
But we made it then and we can make it now
If you believe in me, like I believe in you
We'll find strength in love, we can see this through.

And I'm never gonna let go, never gonna let go
Of these feelings that I have for you,
I only wanna show, I wanna make sure you know
That this love for you is forever yours.

HERE'S YOUR LOVE SONG

ANOTHER LOVE SONG FOR MY WIFE JUANITA. The song itself is upbeat. I hope to record all these songs soon. I wrote this song in our early years of marriage as well. Babe, even after 45 years of marriage I love you more than the day I wrote this song.

Here's Your Love Song

(1980)

In the morning when I wake up, and I see you lying there
I realize my dreams come true as I gently stroke your hair
And you softly call my name; my life will never be the same
But how can I tell you, how much I love you?

So I wrote you this love song, to tell you how I feel,
Yes, I wrote you this love song, to say you are the only one,
To tell you that my heart and soul surround you
My love for you has just begun,
Here's your love song, here's your love song.

In the evening when I come home after working hard all day
It's the little things you do for me, that tell me love is real,
Then you gently take my hand, your
love's so easy to understand.
But how can I tell you, how much I love you
So I wrote you this love song, to tell you how I feel,
Yes I wrote you this love song, to say you are the only one
To tell you that my heart and soul surround you
My love for you has just begun,
Here's your love song, here's your love song.

JANEE

J ANEE IS OUR FIRSTBORN, but the second child. The pregnancy of our first child ended in a miscarriage. Juanita woke me up at 6:00 a.m. to inform me that her water broke. She wasn't due for another three weeks, but Janee had a different plan with her own timeline. Juanita was in labor for 36 hours and began developing complications. She was running a high fever and an infection. Her delivery doctor said she was going to have to do this C-section. Her doctor noticed me trying to look over the shoulders of all the doctors and she asked me if I wanted to see this. I said yes. She told the doctors to step aside and let dad in. Watching Janee being pulled out of Juanita's womb was the most amazing thing I had ever seen. Tears welled up in my eyes. Little did I know this would not be the only time Janee would make me cry, (just kidding Janee). Some tests were run on Janee and they found she had the infection passed to her by Juanita. Janee was in the newborn intensive care unit (NICU) for ten days. The delivery doctor saw me staring at Janee after she had settled in and she said to me, "You might as well ask her what kind of car she wants now because she has you wrapped around her little finger."

I had been at the hospital for almost forty-eight hours when I got home around midnight. I was exhausted and I sat down and cried tears of joy and worry. I pulled out my guitar and wrote this song for her and about her. My dear friend Peg Sosh, known as Aunt Peg, sang the song at Janee's baptism. I love you *mi hija*. You have been a blessing to me your whole life. You helped me run my business, especially when I was in the hospital. You were so good at talking to my customers. They all loved you. And now that I have Parkinson's disease you are my strength and support that keeps me going.

My fondest memory of Janee is why she was given the name "The Negotiator." On all the trips we went to Disneyland or SeaWorld, I always bought the kids something from the gift shops. I always gave them a spending limit of $15. So the kids would spend the day looking at all the different shops, then Janee would come to me to negotiate. Now, my son Andrew was there also. Janee came to me and Andrew stood about five feet back to wait to see what the end price of Janee's negotiations would be. Janee would say, "Well I found this one thing for $14 but I found another thing also and the two of them together are $19." I always gave in. I was a sucker and Janee knew it. Andrew now knew that he had $19 to spend because Janee had negotiated a better deal. Janee has always known how to handle me, and now she knows how to handle me in my serious medical condition. The Negotiator now talks to my doctors about my treatment.

Janee

(1988)

Oh Janee this song's for you,
You are so beautiful if I may say
I hope you know I love you
I'll always be here for you,
You are the sun that lights my day
Oh Janee I thank God for you
You're an answered prayer, a gift from God,
I hope you know He loves you,
He'll always be there for you,
He made all my dreams come true.

Every time that you smile at me
You make me melt,
Every time that your eyes meet mine
I thank God I'm alive.

Oh Janee, Grandma cared for you
She was so thrilled when you said "Agoo,"
I hope you know she loved you
Keep her in your heart with you,
You brought joy to her last days
Oh Janee this song's for you...

ANDREW

FROM DAY ONE, ANDREW WAS A BLESSING to the Sierra household. He approached each day as a new adventure. I loved watching his reactions to new experiences. Andrew hated having his hair washed and going to the dentist. We had to wait until the last minute to tell him these events were about to happen. At about age three the family went up to the Pinal Mountains to play in the snow. I still have a picture of Andrew holding a snowball in his hands and he was so amazed by it. His first experience in the snow was typical of Andrew; he was experiencing a new adventure.

The Sierra family embarked on Disneyland trips and San Diego trips at least twice a year for many years. Janee and Andrew loved Disneyland. I have so many fond memories of these trips. I can still see the look of amazement on Andrew's face the first time he experienced the ocean and the beach. The memory always brings a smile to my face.

Andrew took to music like a fish to water. I tried to teach him the guitar, but after about five lessons I knew I had to find him a more advanced teacher. At the age of thirteen, he played in the band my brother and I had and he had a solo in one song. The solo he played that night blew us all away. It blew me away. I had no idea he could play like that. Little did I know that in just a few years he would steal my job as lead guitarist in another band.

Andrew, you never cease to amaze me with your musical talent. I am so proud of you and your accomplishments in playing multiple instruments. Thank you for the joy you have brought to my life. I love you *mi hijo*.

Andrew

(2021)

The last Sierra child born to the Sierra family
He was a blessing who was amazed with his surroundings,
It was unknown to me at this early time
That this blessing would steal my lead guitarist job.

Andrew's first experience with snow
Was a joy to watch
He and Janee played together in the snow
Now a memory that makes me smile.

Andrew made a snowball and held it out to admire it
He was proud and amazed by his creation,
I still have a photo of this event in his life
Another cherished memory.

Andrew took to music like a fish with water
He excelled rapidly in his ability
At the age of seventeen
He stole my job as lead guitarist.

Andrew was our drummer
And one day after a rehearsal

I told him to play some blues for the guys
All the band members said, "He is our new lead guitarist."

I wasn't angry, in fact, I was proud
I played lead guitar for many years
Now it was his turn,
He tells me that was the best time of his life.

Now I have Parkinson's and I cannot play guitar
I cannot play music with my son,
And it makes me so sad
So I created a new plan for Andrew and me.

We are going to record the many songs I've written
With Andrew playing all the instruments,
I will introduce Andrew to the music community
And give Andrew my final musical gift.

We've come a long way from the day this child said to me,
"Dad there are two worlds, the world we all live in
And the world you live in where you are
the world-famous Gil Sierra."
Mi hijo you are about to enter my world.

TAKE THE TIME

THIS IS A SONG I WROTE ABOUT MY GODSON David Remos. I used to love to spend time with David when he was a toddler. I had a camera and I used to dress him up in costumes and take his picture. David never complained. I think he liked it. Our favorite thing to do was to watch Tom and Jerry. I would sit him on my lap and together we watched Tom and Jerry faithfully every day. We experienced some bad feelings within the family and I became separated from them, and especially David. I wrote this song because I was sad because of all the things in his life I would miss. I was there to watch him destroy his first birthday cake, but I was afraid I would miss his first day of school, graduations, having kids... So I wrote this song describing what I imagined those moments would be like with the hopes that one day David would hear the song and realize how much I love him.

At one time I was the music director at St. Andrew's Catholic Church. I played this song for my choir and the Priest heard it. He was ecstatic. He loved children and he sang the praises of the substance of that song. He instructed me to play the song at the next Mass and he built a sermon around it. David was about ten years old at the time. Juanita invited the whole family to attend Mass that day and they all came. The whole family got to hear the song and David really loved that a song was written about him. That set the family on the road towards forgiveness and healing. I played that song at David's wedding and told the story of why I wrote it. No one in the family had ever heard the story behind the song because I never told anyone. I sang the song and there was not a dry eye in the house. David came over and hugged me after I sang the song and said, "I love you nino." There were tears in his eyes.

A little sidebar here; I wrote the first stanza by myself and played it for my dear friend Peg Sosh and together we finished writing the song in ten minutes.

To David Remos, my godson: I love you and I will always love you as if you are my own son. I am so proud of you and happy for you that you have a beautiful family.

Take the time

(1986)

Take the time to spend some time with someone young
They are the innocence we've lost along the way,
In taking time it shows you care, in caring you give love
It is the love you give that helps them
through each day, each year.

Talk about the seventh wonder of the world
Davey's got a tooth, hey look at that kid smile
Davey made a mess of his first birthday cake
But boy did he have fun and so did everyone.

Take the time to spend some time with someone young
They are the innocence we've lost along the way,
In taking time it shows you care, in caring you give love
It is the love you give that helps them
through each day, each year.

I shed a tear as he climbs the bus
For his first day at school
But felt the joy when he
Came home with his new friend
The tears well up as he leaves again.

He's in college now
Oh, how time has flown,
He's out there on his own.

Take the time to spend some time with someone young
They are the innocence we've lost along the way,
In taking time it shows you care in caring you give love
It is the love you give that helps them
through each day, each year.

I cuddle Davey Jr. in my arms today
I thought of all the words that I used to say,
Now I see the love in Davey as he holds his son,
He's learned as I have learned the key to staying young.

Take the time to spend some time with someone young
They are the innocence we've lost along the way,
In taking time it shows you care, in caring you give love
It is the love you give that helps them
through each day, each year.

VAYA MÉXICO

I WROTE THIS SONG FOR ONE OF MY CHILDREN'S CHOIRS. It is a description of heaven. In Christ's teachings, He always said to let the children come forward. On several occasions, He said that to enter heaven one must have the innocence of a child. The song refers to the children meeting in the village square and the village people meeting them there. The village people are the angels and saints, and together they celebrate and sing joyfully.

Vaya México

(1985)

There is a little town down in Mexico
A little town where the children go
They like to go there cause the people are so kind
And this is what they sing

Vaya, vaya, vaya, vaya con amor,
Vaya, vaya, vaya, vaya con amor.

The children gather in the village square
The village people they meet them there
With hands together they sing and dance
To their favorite melody

Vaya, vaya, vaya, vaya con amor,
Vaya, vaya, vaya, vaya con amor.

Now come you children both young and old
Now you know how the story's told
But if you go there you better be prepared
To join them in this song
Vaya, vaya, vaya, vaya con amor,
Vaya, vaya, vaya, vaya con amor.

Free

(2021)

I woke up today
To a brand-new day
Of healing
And peace.

I had a relationship
That was causing
Harm and hurt
To my family,

I attempted to
Continue the relationship
For many years
But I finally sought closure.

The person will not
Acknowledge, discuss
Or take responsibility
For the hurt and pain to my family,

So today I chose my family
Today I ended that relationship

I will not tolerate anyone
Who chooses to hurt my family.

Yes today is a new day
With the relief of letting go
Today I am healed
Today I am at peace.

LIVING WITH
PARKINSON'S DISEASE

LIVING WITH PARKINSON'S DISEASE

(2021)

THIS CHAPTER IS A COLLECTION OF POEMS I have written documenting my experience of having Parkinson's disease. The purpose of these poems is threefold. First, the poems are intended to educate the community of what those of us with Parkinson's and multiple sclerosis (MS) experience on a daily basis. Second, the poems document my struggles and experience with coping daily with this neurological disorder. Third, these poems seek to encourage anyone who is struggling with some affliction in their lives to fight and not give up.

I was first diagnosed with Parkinson's disease in the summer of 2020, but it was determined that it emerged in January of 2020. When the words came out of the neurologist that I had Parkinson's, my heart sank. I knew immediately that my life is to be forever changed. I called my wife Juanita before I drove off from the office and told her the diagnosis. I cried when I told her and Juanita was silent for a while. When Juanita finally spoke, she said that we will get through this together. I asked her to tell Janee because I didn't feel I could tell her. Juanita said she cried. Andrew was upset as well when I told him. We all knew that Parkinson's is a progressive disease with some life-changing symptoms.

The poems show a progression of my thinking and acceptance of this cross I must carry. The first poem was my realization and sadness of the fact that I would not be able to accomplish so many of the dreams I had. It expresses my sadness in the reality that I will not be able to provide for my family as I did in the past. I also came to realize that I must place my life in God's hands and in the care of my family. The last line states that I will fight and not give up.

Welcome to the journey known as Parkinson's disease.

Reality sinks in

I have so much to live for
I have so much to be grateful for
The people close to me
Make sacrifices for me every day.

I feel undeserving
I feel I have failed
I have so many dreams
Unfulfilled cause I ran out of time.

I was supposed to take care of you
And provide for your future
But you spent a lifetime
Taking care of me instead.

I wish I could do it all over
There are so many things I would change
But since I can't
I can only promise to keep fighting.

Your love for me gives me strength
Your faith in me gives me hope
You make me feel like I can do this
I won't give up.

Daily struggles

Worry, stress, anxiety
And tremors that just won't quit,
Another day in the life
With Parkinson's.
Stress makes the tremors worse
Tremors make the anxiety more intense,
My family has to watch me suffer
I know it makes them worry.

I try to focus on other's trials
Whose pain is worse than mine
I pray for them every day
Asking God to ease their pain.
I fear that if those close to me
Knew how bad it gets sometimes
It would cause them stress, worry, and anxiety,
So I act like I'm fine.

So God, I come to you now
Asking for grace and mercy
Cause I still believe in miracles
I believe that you will save me.

I will wait my turn

Heavenly Father, it's just so hard
The tremors are getting worse
When I'm alone you see me cry
Because I'm afraid,
I've dealt with trauma all my life
Knowing that it always gets worse
Before it gets better
But this worse is hard to bear.

You have been my strength
My whole life for sure
You've carried me through the hardest times
I really need you now, please take my hand
Calm the tremors and calm my fears
Lift me up and dry my tears
Teach me to live day by day
With faith that you will heal me.

Meanwhile, let me offer my suffering
For others who suffer more than I
Grant them healing Lord
Grant them peace...
I can wait my turn.

Deanna, my friend, my inspiration

When I first met her
I was immediately amazed
By her piano skills
And music sight reading skills,

I felt unworthy to approach her
My musicianship
Was significantly below
Her music ability and knowledge.

The day I met her
I was pleasantly surprised
She was approachable
She was a gentle soul,

We spent days and days
Talking about music
I played guitar
In her church choir,

We wrote an instrumental piece
Together and recorded it,
One of my most memorable
Recording sessions.

I introduced her to the family
We adopted her as one of us
She and her son
Celebrate Thanksgiving with us.

I remember the day
I took her to the hospital
For a spinal tap
The doctors suspected MS,

We got the news
And my senses were overwhelmed
But from day one
She has been so brave,

Throughout the years
She never complained
She researched and asked questions
And was proactive in her treatment.

Eventually she was unable to keep
A full time job.
Because the heat is tough on MS
She spends half the year up north.

Despite her pain and challenges
She is very supportive

Concerning my Parkinson's symptoms
Because some of our symptoms are similar.

So once again I stand in amazement
Of this incredible soul,
She inspires me, she shares her strength
You are my hero, my friend,
Forever I will love and cherish you.

Encouragement from a friend

God spoke to me today
He sent me a message
Through a good friend and brother
That I haven't seen for several years,

My friend sounded hurt and troubled
He said, brother, I'm sorry I haven't called
But it hurts so much to see you like this
It just can't be true, it's not you,

Parkinson's is not you
You are full of life and love
We are supposed to play more music together
But alas it's not to be,

You are God's warrior
Even though your suffering
You are strong, loving, and caring,
I look up to you.

His words opened my heart
To realize that those close to me
Are hurting also to have to see

Me like this every day,

I now understand that my extended family members

Are not ignoring me

They are simply struggling

To see me like this.

Yes, God spoke to me today,

He said I am loved and I am cherished,

He surrounded me with earth angels who care about me,

I am truly blessed.

TO LUKE OZGA,
MY NINE-YEAR-OLD HERO

I KNEW OF LUKE THROUGH MY WIFE JUANITA because she works with Luke's mother, Heather. I remember when Luke was first diagnosed with cancer and Heather had to quit her job to take care of Luke full time. Luke has spent countless days in the hospital combatting this cancer and other side effects and symptoms. With the help of his brother Josh, Luke has beaten cancer two times. Josh has provided bone marrow for Luke's treatment. Alas, after going into remission twice, cancer has reemerged with a vengeance. Heather is told that Luke's last hope is an experimental treatment in Texas. At the time of writing the poem, Luke had not yet been accepted in the experimental treatment. Since then he has been accepted into the trial.

The inspiration for this poem came from a local news story. A local news station interviewed Heather and Luke. Heather explained the struggles of the journey, the highs and lows, and spoke of this last chance treatment. You could see the concern for Luke on Heather's face. You could see her struggle to maintain her composure. Heather said that Luke told her, "I don't want to die." Heather wanted to cry when she said that but she didn't. I did though. Dear God, have mercy on this mother who must hear those words from her son. The words that Luke spoke next are the inspiration for this poem. Luke said, "If you want to succeed, you have to stay strong." Brave and wise words from a young child.

To Luke Ozga, my nine-year-old hero

God sent me an angel
In the form of a child
Fighting for his life
In a battle against cancer,

Today he faces
His last hope chance
In an experimental treatment
Far away from home.

I see the struggle and fear
In his mother's eyes
And hear the pain
In her voice,

She must hear her child say
"I don't want to die,"
While she is overcome
With helplessness.

His cancer is rare
There is no known treatment or protocol
There is only faith, hope,
And God's mercy.

The reality of the Parkinson's
That I have is that
It is progressive
And can lead to dementia and death.

My fears are similar in that
I don't want to die like that
I too live by faith and hope
And pray for God's mercy,

So God sent me an angel
In the form of a young child
Who spoke God's message:
"If you want to succeed, you must stay strong."

Lord, bless and heal this child
And messenger
Of faith, hope, and determination,
Give him strength and help him to be strong.

The world can be cruel

My wife and daughter
Work two jobs
They are exhausted,
So I did the grocery shopping.

It is difficult to navigate
An inconsiderate world
As a person
With a serious disability.

Approaching the door
In the crosswalk
Anyone can see by the way I walk
That there is something wrong with me,

Ten people approaching the door
Speed up when they see me
To get to the door before me
So that I don't slow them down,

I was at the door, almost in
When one last person
Rushes passed me,

Instead of respectfully waiting for me.
In the produce section
I am very slow at performing tasks
Because the tremors
Cause coordination problems.

A young man in his thirties
Gives me a look of disgust,
And his body language said
I am inconveniencing him.

Pushing my cart slowly
Through the store
I felt like I was driving slowly
In the left lane of the freeway,

Shopping carts passing me
To the left and the right
Giving me dirty looks
As they went by.

I don't want to sound
Angry or bitter
Or deserving of special treatment,
But it's obvious there is something wrong with me.

So to those people in Safeway,
So impatient and inconsiderate,
I wasn't there for you,
I was taking care of my family
So get over yourselves.

I'll pray for you

I will lay myself to sleep now
Sleep is the only escape from the tremors,
The Parkinson's was bad today
Discouragement crept in.

It's getting more difficult to walk
I'm losing my balance more often
I almost fell down today
But my will won out, I stayed upright.

I'm a fighter
I don't know how to give up
I'm a believer
That I am surrounded by angels.

Tomorrow is another day
There is so much to do
There are so many to pray for
To help them get through.

All the prayers needed
For babies who are sick
Children with cancer

People scared with COVID-19

Open heart surgeries

Relatives in car accidents

Depression running ramped

A world in despair.

So I will rest tonight

So I can awake

To pray for you again

Because I care about you,

My brothers and sisters

Be not afraid

Walk in faith and trust

And know that I love you too.

COVID-19

THE ICU NURSE

WITH ALL THE COVID-19 STORIES in the news, there are real people, real faces, and real pain and sorrow being experienced. The ICU Nurse poem was written about a nurse who was crying, telling her story of what it is like on the front line of COVID-19. The story told in this poem is the story she told in the news. She shared this sad and heartbreaking experience and I am sharing it with you. This poem is dedicated to and to honor all the frontline nurses and doctors who fight this COVID-19 virus every day, and fight the fatigue and emotional stress it causes. God bless you.

The ICU Nurse

(2021)

I cried today
Just like yesterday
With more tears to come tomorrow.

She was a mother of three
Of two boys and one girl
Just like me,

She put up a fight
But her body grew weak
She didn't make it through the night,

I stayed with her
I held her hand
I was the last person she saw.

So now I cry
As another dies
And it hurts so much inside,

I'll be back tomorrow
With a heart filled with sorrow
Dear God have mercy on us.

TO PEG SOSH,
MY BELOVED FRIEND

A T THE TIME OF THIS WRITING, the death toll from COVID-19 was reported at 700,000. It is so easy to grow callous of the deaths and forget a very important fact. Each one of those deaths was a life that was lived and cut short. How easy it is to forget that those lives will no longer contribute to our society. They will never love again, or be loved. Lest we forget that for each death there was a life, this poem tells the story of one of those lives that was taken by COVID-19. A life that meant very much to me. A person who is loved and missed.

To Peg, my beloved friend

(2021)

How do I begin
To tell the story
Of a lifetime
Of friendship and love.

My first memory
Is my freshman year
Cruising Globe with three senior girls,
Peg, Bertha, and Louise.

You graduated and left Miami
I didn't see you for several years
But when you returned
We reconnected through music.

Peg, you were the original wedding singer,
A legend in Miami,
Every bride wanted you to sing at their wedding,
I was along for the ride.

Everyone complimented your beautiful voice,
My guitar seemed to know

How to play and sound
To make you sound better.
We formed a trio
"Gil, Peg, and Bill,"
Weekends at Angel's Pizza
And a couple of concerts at MHS.

We were in a band together
"Sierra CT Express,"
You were compared to Sade
Your voice penetrated the soul.

"Smooth Operator," "Careless Whispers,"
"Hello" by Lionel Ritchie,
A few of my favorite songs
I loved to hear you sing.

Together we wrote a song,
"Take the Time,"
About my godson David Remos,
I promise I will record it.

You recorded the vocals
On the song for Danny Rios,
To this day I am amazed
At the professionalism of your voice.

The band changed direction
You chose to leave the band,
That was a really sad ending
To the beautiful sound of a songbird.

I lost interest in music
'Cause you were no longer there,
Music was empty
It lost its purpose.

We were separated once again
Your health began to fail
You wanted your privacy,
I felt so helpless.

You knew me better than anyone
You helped me through
The pain and struggles
In my life.

To Janee you are Aunt Peg
To Andrew you are Nina
To Juanita and me you are
Friend and counselor.

Many have failed to
Document a lifetime
Of experiences in a poem
But we did.

A gentle soul
A loving, loyal friend
You are missed and loved
Until we meet again
And play music together.

CONCLUSION

LAST THOUGHTS

TO A PERSON WITH A DISABILITY, the world can be cruel, unforgiving, impatient, and inconsiderate. Avoid becoming angry and bitter because there are many caring, loving, accepting, and generous people in our society as well. Look around you, your friends and family are praying for you. Never give up hope. Put your faith and trust in God. Like Luke says, "If you want to succeed, you have to stay strong."

I hope this book encourages you to find the resilience to move forward with your life. Do not mourn what you have lost, but reinvent yourself. Find your new purpose in life. Be encouraged by the experiences in this book. The migrants from El Salvador were desperate for their lives and took a chance to escape the death they faced at home. They may have died, but they showed courage and did not give up. The children who believed in their project to help Nikki White did so with love, determination, and purpose. Learn from these children and have the courage to face obstacles and adversity like they did. The purpose of a generation of Mexican Americans who received poor treatment in Miami, Arizona was to provide a better life for their children. And they succeeded. A whole generation of Mexican Americans from Miami went to college because of the sacrifices of their parents. Instead of being angry, bitter, and discouraged that generation created change for the next generation.

My personal story of Parkinson's is that I lost the ability to play the guitar. I can no longer write songs to play on my guitar. I began expressing my feelings and experiences in poems and found a new purpose. Look at me, I just wrote a book of poems and I am in the process of writing another book entitled *Mexican American Servant Leaders from Miami, Arizona.* Reinvent yourself and find your new purpose. Never give up hope. I would like to share the wisdom of my daughter Janee when she was seven years old. I was in a deep depression. On this particular day, I had decided my family would be better off without me and was contemplating suicide. Janee came to me with a piece of paper and said, "I wrote a poem for you daddy." The poem read, "In the sky there are angels, if you don't believe just look up." My seven-year-old daughter was telling me to have faith. Learn to have the faith of a child.

Lastly, pray for one another. I pray for you every day. I don't know who you are, but God does and he knows I'm praying for you. Never lose faith in the power of prayer. Accept the love and help from those around you. They are sincere from their heart in their desire to help you. Chances are before your disability you reached out to help others. Now it is your turn to accept the love and support from the people who love you. You are loved and don't forget it. Go in peace with God's grace and blessings.

ABOUT THE AUTHOR

GILBERT LUNA SIERRA is a happily married man to his high school sweetheart for forty-six years. He knows he is a happily married man because his wife tells him so every day. He grew up in the small mining town of Miami, Arizona, with small-town values and big hopes and dreams.

The author had a successful forty-five-year career as a Tile Contractor and is now embarking on a second career as an author. He is a musician, songwriter, recording artist, sound/recording engineer, and music recording producer. He played the guitar for fifty-seven years and has written songs for thirty-five years.

The focus of his endeavors changed in 2020 when he was diagnosed with Parkinson's Disease. The severe tremors in his left hand prevent him from playing the guitar. This harsh new reality encouraged him to write poetry to satisfy his need to create—this first book —and the many more to come. This new gift has provided much-needed release from the fears and anxieties brought on by Parkinson's Disease.

The author obtained a master's degree in Leadership, which began his experience of researching and writing. While in the doctoral program, the author became interested in phenomenological research, which served him well because, as it turns out, as an author, he is telling stories rather than researching and coming to scientific conclusions.

His name, Gilbert Luna Sierra, honors his mother's family and father's family. It serves to celebrate the Mexican culture he grew up with, emphasizing family unity, including the extended family. He learned from the struggles and sacrifices of his parent's generation, and the lessons learned are helping him cope with Parkinson's Disease. An illustration of this is when a friend asked him, "How are you doing? I don't mean for you to just tell me, 'Fine,' I want to know how you really are with Parkinson's getting worse." The author's response was, "Parkinson's is progressing. The tremors are more severe. Stability and balance are a problem, and it is just a matter of time before I fall. But I refuse to let Parkinson's symptoms dictate how I feel." The author refuses to allow Parkinson's Disease to stop him from contributing value to society.

BOOK, FOLLOW, OR MESSAGE THE AUTHOR

Forthcoming Soundtrack Summer 2022:
"Thoughts to Heal Your Soul"

Website:
GilbertLunaSierraAuthor.com

**Follow author on Facebook for updates
on his music and writings:**
Facebook.com/Gilbert-Luna-Sierra-Author-100540589132567

www.ingramcontent.com/pod-product-compliance
Lightning Source LLC
Chambersburg PA
CBHW020919140626
46545CB00015B/945